Finding the
Joy
In Cancer

Rev. Allen Mosley

BALBOA
PRESS

A DIVISION OF HAY HOUSE

Balboa Press books may be ordered through booksellers or by contacting:

Balboa Press
A Division of Hay House
1663 Liberty Drive
Bloomington, IN 47403
www.balboapress.com
1-(877) 407-4847

Because of the dynamic nature of the Internet, any web addresses or links contained in this book may have changed since publication and may no longer be valid. The views expressed in this work are solely those of the author and do not necessarily reflect the views of the publisher, and the publisher hereby disclaims any responsibility for them.

The author of this book does not dispense medical advice or prescribe the use of any technique as a form of treatment for physical, emotional, or medical problems without the advice of a physician, either directly or indirectly. The intent of the author is only to offer information of a general nature to help you in your quest for emotional and spiritual well-being. In the event you use any of the information in this book for yourself, which is your constitutional right, the author and the publisher assume no responsibility for your actions.

Any people depicted in stock imagery provided by Thinkstock are models, and such images are being used for illustrative purposes only.

Certain stock imagery © Thinkstock.

Printed in the United States of America

ISBN: 978-1-4525-6817-1 (sc)
ISBN: 978-1-4525-6818-8 (e)

Balboa Press rev. date: 02/11/2013

Table of Contents

Thank you

Two of the greatest words ever created.

I would like to start this thank you process with my Beloved "Honey" Tony, who reminds me each day that taking the journey is worth it. Your constant support and love give me strength and courage on those days it would be easier to hide out.

To my countless friends, who I call family for holding the light in this process. For all the treatments, prayers, rides, food, visits, and for holding my truth with me along the way. To the East Bay International Choir for allowing me to sing with you, and find a new path. To each and everyone who helped birth this with financial support, allowing that in was a great life lesson and thank you for supporting this deam.

To all the friends who held this book complete, and allowed me to shares in the process.

To Kay H Neill and Tony Winsley for taking on the biggest editing job in the world. Words can not express my gratitude and love for your support in this process.

To the Amor Spiritual Center for allowing me to be your Spiritual Leader and live my life in public with you. You are the living proof of this love made manifest.

To my parents for allowing me to be their son and love me for who I am.

I love you
Rev. Allen Mosley

Chapter One:

What's Eating me?

You know when you play the victim role all your life, you start collecting data for the next big role. I imagine it is like an actor who does research for the next role they're reading for. I was busy planning my next role, my best role ever. I was going to get the Oscar for best victim or it was going to kill me.

I love this definition of Cancer from The Dream Book by Bethards

> "Anger, Frustration, Disappointment; fear eating away inside you. Lack of self-love; inability to look at inner disharmony or refusal to do so. Suppression of any kind is dangerous to physical, mental and emotional health; verbalize, get things up and out, be honest with yourself."

Be honest with myself, were they kidding? I didn't even know myself. Oh I had read the book and played the roles. I had become a master at looking like I had it all together from the outside when the whole time my inside was being eaten away.

It was one of those "rubber meets the road" places. I had a choice to continue on that path, or breathe life into my internal filing system, the very fiber of my being. I could continue to blame everyone else for my hurt and pain or I could take responsibility for my part in it all and change my life. Old path extinction, new path freedom and the unknown. I didn't know at the time if this would be enough to save me from extinction, I was seeing how I had allowed fear, resentment, and anger to consume my life. Have you ever met someone who seemed really nice and yet there was that something within you that was telling you things are not as they appeared. That was me. I knew that I had always been a loving and kind person. I was willing to give you the shirt off my back. I was willing to be your best friend. I was willing to be whoever you needed me to be as long as you would love me the way I wanted to be loved. Mind you, I didn't know how that was. I had some made up story of happily ever after. Yet it seemed time and time again "YOU" would screw it up, and I would be there holding the bag, telling anyone who would listen "See I told you so!" I could have received an Oscar for best victim playing that role...Best "Victim" goes to... me, me, pick me!

I was so in love with the image of love, what it looked like, and how it should be - I didn't really want to know what I needed to do to get there. I was going to make it happen. With each romantic encounter I was telling myself "I'm not enough", and for years I had closed my heart to any hope of romance, instead I would go out to meet my sexual needs in whatever means necessary. With each encounter I would file the hurt, pain, and self hatred deeper and deeper in the cells and tissues of my body, never intending to look at those files again. This was not a new experience, it had started very early in my life. I learned that giving people what they wanted sexually would insure they wanted me around.

I know this may sound very odd coming from a male perspective. After all, we are programmed from an early age to conquer and get the next notch on the bed post of life. Here I was as a very young boy knowing that all I really wanted was someone to spend time with me and touch me in a loving way. If I couldn't have that, I would give myself away sexually to have physical touch; even if it was to be kept a secret. A secret of shame I was filing in the cells of my body. It was a belief I chose to be my truth. Who I was and where my worth came from was in my ability to please and pleasure others; my needs and wants didn't matter or count. I learned this belief system at an early age and I learned to play the role well. Here I was in my 40's still giving myself away anywhere, anyhow. I was hiding the hurt, pain, and hate in the cells of my body, feeding the malignant growths that I would soon find out where eating me alive.

It wasn't important to me that I had cancer; I knew that was a symptom of a much greater truth. It was important to find what was eating me alive. It was time for me to find the files that contained the hurt, the pain, the anger, and all the things I had stuffed down deep in the tissues of my body and breathe breath into them again. I had to release them if I ever hoped to find life again.

Chapter Two:

Hidden Beliefs

I know that the medical team would do what they had to do and I knew my work was to relieve the hurt that had been consuming my body from the inside out. I had become so good at "looking good" and pleasing others that I was unwilling to spend any time alone with myself. I didn't even really know who I was and if I would like whom I found on this search to joy. The one thing I did know from what I was reading, and from the New Thought classes was that if I wanted a change; it had to start with me. I knew that the years of pretending were up. If I didn't change my thinking and how I was living my life I would die. I knew I wanted to live, and I wanted to change, yet I was terrified of spending one on one time with myself, let alone listening to the voice of God, who had hated me from birth.

I had so many beliefs about myself that were hateful that I had hidden. I had to find them and choose which truths were actually true and which no longer served me. I had to choose new thoughts and I had to do this NOW. I had to ask myself "what is my truth?" I didn't know... I didn't even know who I was, I had been a puppet, a chameleon for so long I didn't know who I was, let alone would I like myself. The thought of loving myself and speaking my truth scared me to death. Yet I knew I had two clear choices as I saw it, I could stay on the path I was on and die a victim, or I could start the journey to loving myself and finding joy in my life. Whatever the outcome, it was up to me. I had to do the heavy lifting of discovering who I was and finding a way to love that little boy locked inside of me.

As I looked back over my life I realized there was one common denominator in all of my experiences. ME. I took a look at myself with new glasses, outside of the ego and what it had told me throughout my entire life. "If they had..." "Life will be better when"... "I had no part in this...", this is not my fault..." I sat there in this beautiful apartment, an amazing visual for the world to see that I had it all together and I was somebody, while inside my body was eating itself to extinction. I realized that I had bought into the lie that what really matters is what others think of you and how you look to the outside world.

Oh, I could stand there and say I was living the good life and from the outside view I was indeed, yet I forgot to send the memo to the inside of my body. You know the places and crevasses within my life where I had stuffed all the pain, hurt, self hatred, not good enough, not smart enough, too fat, too...

All of my life I held the image of God as this bearded man in the heavens, who, at any moment, could and would punish you for some unknown reason that you had not lived up to His version of what He expected. I had also lived with the belief system that my being who I was as a person was indeed insuring my path to hell. My intention in this part of the book is to suggest you find your own path of awakening. This is mine and today I realize it was a path I had been on for years. I was a good southern boy who had been raised in church and to be honest it was the most amazing place on earth until I was 16 years old. It was the safe space, where I was able to shine and where "who I was mattered." I had been singing as early as I could open my mouth. I was the welcome committee and meeting a new person was a friend yet to be. When I sang I felt the closest to my understanding of connection to something bigger than me. I had sung in church since I was 3 years old.

My mom tells the story that we would go to church and she would sit me on the pew and I would turn around and sing to everyone behind me. I remember being in the choir standing in the front corner looking out singing with all my heart. From my boyhood perspective, it was heaven on earth. It was the one time I felt I had my dad's attention in a good way. I felt that I was doing something that made him proud of me. I have always been a singer. I had voice lessons instead of going with the rest of the teenagers up to the local hang out. My voice was my connection and I loved being in the place of calm and peace where it was just God and I standing together enjoying the love.

At age 16 is when my parents found out that I was not the young man they had raised and my life changed forever. Outside of church, my mom had been my best friend. I knew that no matter what, I would always have her on my side in life. That all changed one day when she listened to my recorded singing about being in love. I remember it so very clearly. The person I had told almost everything to in my life was asking me about love. We were sitting at the kitchen table with my sister and in the revealing of my true self, she asked me about marriage. I said it will not happen, she asked how I could say that. I said not to a woman at least. I had never seen my mom cry before that day and I knew that "I" had broken something in her that would never heal. I lost my best friend in the world. From that day forward we kept a secret; my mom, my sister, and I. Hoping against hope that my dad would never find out who his little boy had grown up to be.

The shame of that time in my life was great and I found the perfect way to heal it, I started hanging out with the old high school friends and hiding who I really was. One night a group of guys got together and for the first time I had to choose "to be cool and drink, or be outside yet again." For the first time in my life I drank and smoked until I blacked out. That was the night I had someone put a gun to my head and want to kill me; I had made a pass at him in a drunken state. Within weeks my dad found out and I was without a place to call home. I spent the next while drowning my sorrows in a bottle and looking for someone to love me for being me. Now being 17 years of age that was very easy to do. By the time I was 18 I had learned a lesson of a lifetime. I was the only thing I could count on in life, and everyone that I loved would leave. As a child age three I had a best friend. She was my aunt and everyday she would get off the school bus after school and come and spend time with me. It was amazing. I had someone who loved me and spent all this time with me. I was in heaven. Between Aunt Jodie and mom I had everything I ever needed. I had love around me at all times and I was safe. When I was four or five my best friend got married and all I knew was she liked him more than me (not good enough) and she went away and I didn't see her for a long time. This was the belief system I had put into place as a child to deal with this hurt and to not allow it to happen again.

When I was age 6 and it was time to go to school my other best friend took me to this strange place and left me there. I cried for weeks and weeks. The teacher didn't know what to do with me.

My mom tells this story.

> "I had tried everything to help you adjust to school telling you to be a big boy for mama, and big boys don't cry. I would tell you I needed you to be a big boy and not cry at school any more. One day you come home from school running in the house smiling and I thought finally he found a way to be happy at school. I asked, how was school today, and you said I learned an amazing thing at school today mama. What is that honey? I learned that the bathroom is a great place to cry."

I had learned these truths about my life by the age of 6.

"When you love someone they always leave. Do what makes other feel good and they will like you, and play with you. Hide your emotions because real boys don't cry."

These beliefs would play themselves out over and over again in my life. In every breakup, I would hide the pain and hurt in the cells and tissue of my body. I would continue to give myself away in order to have others "play" with me. I would only cry when I was alone and I would sob and be ashamed of myself in the process. These are the beliefs I had to find and uncover in order to change the path I was on. I realize today that I held that same truth about God, for I had loved that bearded man and I sang my songs only to him, and now, he didn't want me either.

I had spent most of my adult life "playing" with this figure I called God and I wanted to get to the bottom of it once and for all. I had heard all the stories from childhood about folks' faith being tested and just when it was going good "BAM"!! Smack over the head and back to the beginning of the line for you.

I continued to sing and hide the parts of myself that I didn't want my bearded friend to know about, and had even gone so far as to ask for His support in finding "the one." Only to find that once I loved them they would leave. I learned how to separate love from sex, I learned how to give what I needed to get what I wanted. I had learned how to survive in the world, yet at what cost? Every hurt, pain, anger, resentment, and fear I had stuffed deep down inside of me never to be looked at again. Through countless STD's, HIV, drugs, alcohol, trails, and back seats, I kept telling myself that I was not good enough and that when you love someone they leave. So more times than not I would leave first. I had learned the path of survival and I was never going to be hurt again.

Here I was sitting in the living room that I had created; looking for the answers on what was eating me and where to begin. I was alone and rather than take on myself at that moment I took on God. I wanted to know who this person was and where did I fit into this relationship? I began to realize that I had build this relationship, like every other relationship, with the understanding that I needed to give Him what He wanted and that if I ever fell in love with Him, He would leave me too (not good enough!) Somewhere that night, sitting there in the dark in my living room, I started asking God what the deal was. I remembered when I walked away from this relationship like so many before. I was going to leave God before God left me. I had built the same relationship with God that I had build with every other person I had in my life. Tell them what they want to hear, give them what they ask for and they will stay around.

My wonderful friend Donald Gene, who I met in early recovery from drugs and alcohol, came to mind. We found our way into recovery only a week apart. We were best friends from the get go. It was great! We began to find out more and more about each other and none of it really mattered. We were on a common journey of survival and we needed each other to survive. Over the next year there were three of us that would hang out together Donald, Donald, and me. When it came time for our one year anniversary of sobriety, Donald asked me to sing at his celebration. It was the first time I sang in years. I sang a song called Friends Are Friends Forever. I asked him to share his story at my celebration. It was then that I realized that he was telling my story.

Within a few months of our celebration, Donald became very ill and was hospitalized. Within months, his health was on a decline and we didn't know why. This was in the 80's and we had all been a part of this free love movement. What I know for myself today was that it was really "self hatred of myself."

Within a few months Donald discovered he had this new disease called "AIDS" and that it didn't look good. Here was this man who was beautiful and full of life changing before me. Donald had the most beautiful hair. He had this amazing style and his hair reminded me of Elvis; and I loved him for it. There was never a hair out of place and it always looked great. As the disease began to take more of a hold on his life, Donald found a way to peace and wanted me to have that same peace for myself. We would sit and he would ask me questions. He would say "Saster (his southern drawl for our word sister) why do you hate yourself so much? Here I am fighting to stay alive and you are doing everything you can to kill yourself. You are a good man and you deserve the best. I want that for you, you have everything to live for!"

On one of our many talks over that year, Donald called me one day crying. "Saster can you bring me a beanie for my head, I am losing my hair so I asked Donald to cut it all off." I stopped what I was doing and took him a beanie in the hospital. We hugged and I realized the old exit strategy that had been a part of my life so many times before. "Leave before they leave you." On one of my visits, Donald asked me to promise him something. We went back and forth until I surrendered and promised, which was something that I never did. I then asked what it was he wanted. He stated" I want you to sing for me at my funeral." I stated "NO WAY! I want nothing to do with God, he doesn't love me and I don't love him either. I want nothing to do with him; he is taking you away from me!" Donald in his calm still voice said "Saster, I can't go anywhere in peace until you know that you deserve love and that you matter. Please get that for yourself, and I know you will keep your promise because you are a man of your word." By the time we got to our second year celebration, Donald was in the hospital very ill, and didn't' recognize us on our visits. I remember getting both of our chips that year to celebrate our recovery and taking his to the hospital. This was the first time in weeks that he remembered who I was and he looked me in the eyes and I said "we made it saster, we made it!" He smiled and thanked me and told me that he loved me. It was on that visit

I told him it was ok for him to go, that I was going to be ok. Within hours Donald was on the next journey of his life.

Here I was at another crossroad in my life; one more person that I let in my life had left me. I was mad with God. I was mad with Donald. I was mad with myself for allowing this to happen. And I didn't want to enter the doors of the church to sing for him under any circumstances. Within a week I was sitting in this church called First MCC in Atlanta GA mad, crying, and grieving over one of my best friends. As the service started, I was happy to say the building didn't burn down around me and that lightening had not struck me dead. As I sat there crying and not knowing how I would ever be able to sing for my friend, I had the first honest conversation with God I had ever had. "If you really love me... and really give a damn about me... you will help me sing for my friend, so I can keep my word to him." As I walked to the podium crying the entire way I grabbed the sides of the podium and the tears stopped and I opened my mouth and out came the voice of an angel. The moment the song was over I burst into tears again. I heard these words "We will talk later when you are ready; I love you just the way you are."

I was still very angry and hurt and I didn't know what to make of this whole thing, yet for the first time ever I felt I was safe and I didn't know what to make of it all. But wait, I thought this was a story about cancer and how to find joy in it?

Chapter Three:

The Layers of the Onion

Over the next year I found a new relationship with God and was singing, directing, and spending most of my time at First MCC. I was building a relationship with someone I had never met before. I was finding my way free to look at what was going on within me and dealing with the lies I had believed about myself and others like me. I had been sober for two year and the fog was beginning to clear and I was building this relationship with the thing called "God" who apparently was very different from the one my parents knew. Around this time I began to have suppressed memories, some that I didn't remember, and others that I did very well. I was unlocking the door to my past and allowing some of the secrets to come to the surface. I remember standing in the choir singing and my best friend "Effie" pinched me on the butt in fun. I turned around with tears running down my face and she knew in that moment that it had triggered a memory from the past. She realized that she had hurt me and she was so sad, we both stood there crying and couldn't stop. This went on for weeks. It was affecting my work, my life, my sanity. I didn't understand what was happening to me. My life was falling apart at the seams. One day while at work, one of the staff came into my office to cash out and she asked if she could run energy on me? I didn't know what she was talking about yet I knew I needed relief in the worst way and I said yes. She was working on her masters and told me to give her a call if I ever needed to talk;

the door was always open. The best way I can describe that time in my life is the M&M candies. I had a hard shell for protection, and was soft mushy on the inside. I would burst into tears at any moment, and my old friend, sleep, had become my enemy as I would wake in terror of my memories and dreams.

I was driving down the road one day and the flood gates opened and I found myself parked in the front yard of my co worker knocking at her door asking if we could talk? This began a year and a half of intense therapy. One door would open and another would slam shut. I had shut down emotionally and I was closing everyone out. If anyone tried to touch me, I burst into tears. I would sleep with one leg over the side of the bed so I could run at a moment's notice. This was the journey of being a victim that would haunt me for the next twenty years of my life. I hated everyone from my childhood, all the folks that I had given what they wanted so they would love me in a way I understood. To say that the next year of my life was intense was an understatement! Yet, in the midst of it all, I was building a relationship with a new understanding of myself and God and I wanted to share it with the world. Over the next year of weekly sessions and much personal work I began to see the light at the end of the tunnel. For the first time in my life I was sharing that I had been sexually abused as a child. I thought at the time it was the most shameful thing to ever happen in my life. Though I was dealing with many of the things I had stuffed down inside myself, I realize today that I had found the first layer of the onion.

Moving to the county in rural Alabama was the last thing I ever thought I would do, being "raised" in rural Georgia was a lesson in understanding for a young boy who knew he was very different from the rest of the children. I learned at a very early age about "fitting in" and what that looked like. I learned to hide the parts of myself that didn't please others. I had learned to be a chameleon very well. As part of my self discovery, I began to sing again with the friends I had in Atlanta. This was an amazing space to make music. My wonderful friends: Effie, JR, Victor and I, started singing together. We jokingly called ourselves Mama and Fat Boys. We had such fun and were asked to sing at the 10 year anniversary in Huntsville AL and we said yes. Back in the late 80's, the interstate freeways had not made it to Huntsville yet and I like to say that in order to get to Huntsville, you had to go somewhere else first! Once you got there, you needed to take the back roads to find your way. While in the car with Effie and the boys I recall saying "I would never move there!"

Knowing what I know today about the law of attraction and that which I give out comes back to me, it is no surprise that 3 months later, I was living in Huntsville surrounded by cotton fields. On our visit to Huntsville I met a wonderful man who was very kind and loving. He had come along at a time in my life when I was open to love and loving myself. I had been in therapy for well over a year and cleared out a great deal of hurt and pain. I feel this is a perfect time to talk about "hidden beliefs" or belief systems (BS) as I like to refer to it. No matter how much love anyone showered over me, there was still this belief that I didn't deserve it; that I wasn't good enough for love or for a relationship for that matter. It wasn't long before the BS and the Law of Attraction started manifesting that into reality. I was always doing my best to make up for not being good enough in my head by doing as much as I could to make everything look perfect. We had the perfect house, the perfect cars, and the perfect relationship looking from the outside in. Yet, in my thoughts was this knowing that just like all the folks before, everyone I loved would leave. Coupled with I'm not good enough and knowing my past, we began to become distant and not touch. His work had him traveling more which for me was mini proof of him leaving like all the others over and over again. When he would come home, I had walls built around me so high that no one could find the way over. When on the rare chance he did, it would be short lived as he had to pack and leave on the next trip.

To the outside world we looked amazing: I was very involved in church. I had been voted to the board. I was preaching. I was sharing more about the abuse and how my life had changed. On the inside I was back to my old pattern of behavior, stuffing all the pain down as deep as I could. The pain was not the only thing I would stuff. I was eating everything in sight. I was building a shield of protection around me that would send a clear message to anyone NOT GOOD ENOUGH!!! This continued until one day we had a talk about not being happy and my world came crashing down.

At this point I closed the door on love for many years to come. I didn't even try and if I did it would be very short lived because deep down inside I knew the truth.

A) I wasn't good enough.

B) They were just going to leave anyway.

While in Huntsville and my work with the Church I met a wonderful friend named Keith from North Carolina. He is one of the most gifted musicians I have ever had the pleasure of meeting and that is saying a great deal. Keith taught school and had the summers off and had agreed to go on tour with me for the summer. We took off across the country singing and ministering our way to churches along the way. I had decided that I would put myself into ministry and close the door to love in my life. If I could only save one other person from a life of abuse and pain I would surely make it to heaven with a crown. I would sing and talk about the past as if it was all behind me, and hold that life was great and I was "saved" from a life of hell. The truth is that is the lie I was telling myself and the person I was trying to save was not someone else it was me. Oh I didn't know that at the time, I had moved into savior mode in my life and I was going to save everyone from themselves. I like to look on this time in my life as the "Self Righteous phase." By the end of the tour it is a wonder that Keith would even speak to me, and for a few weeks we didn't. I was out of money, nowhere to go and yep you guessed it ... not good enough. Once again I was mad at my understanding of God and how I had been called out here to do this work and God had not made a way for me to do it.

I was always looking outside of myself for all the answers. I was always holding someone else to blame for all the things going wrong in my life. Always looking for the reason to hate myself even more and hurt myself for being such a bad person. During this time in my life I worked cleaning folks homes, bars, and singing at St. Johns in North Carolina. I was allowing my shadow self to run the show more and more. I had come to the understanding that if I couldn't succeed at ministry, that God didn't want me either I wasn't good enough for that anyway. So I started working at the local bar and found myself giving myself away more and more. I had turned off self love, love from a relationship, and love from others. I was looking for the people in my life that would cause more pain so that I could be punished for being who I was. If I could atone for my sins maybe I could find happiness once again. I had this understanding that if I could turn one bad boy around there was a chance I could be saved as well. So I would find one bad boy after another trying my best to save them even thought they never asked for help and were perfectly happy in their life. Today I know that I had made them bad so that I could save them, thus saving myself. It had nothing to do with them at all. It was my way of continuing to look outside myself and putting all the blame on someone else. I was once again living the victim role. I had become so good at separating love and sex that I began to just enjoy the casual affairs and to go home alone as it was so much easier and safer that way. That way my heart never had to get involved and I could get my needs met.

This is how I lived my life. Working in the bars on Saturday night, giving myself away to wild pleasure and then leading praise and worship on Sunday at St Johns, doing my best to save the bad boy from a life in hell. I was very aware of my life and how I was living. I found myself taking greater and greater risks with my health, and pleasure. I found my way to the leather community. This was just what I needed to feed the pleasure and the punishment of my life. I didn't need anyone else to tell me about my life. I already knew I was prosecutor, judge, and jury. I continued to look for the men who could cause the most harm and hurt me the most. Yet to the outside world I was now very active in the church. I was preaching on a regular basis. I was the steward chair at the church. I was leading praise and worship every week. I was very proud of my life in ministry while hiding the truth of my shadow life from most.

I had won a local title in the leather community and my shadow life was forced out into the open more. Everyone from Church was a bit taken aback yet loved me the same. I remember the pride event that year. I lead the choir in a song on the main stage dressed in leather and jeans and once we were finished I removed my jeans to march in the parade in my chaps and cod piece. The look on the faces of the folks from the church was amazement. I was asked not to march with the church that day so I rode on the float from the bar. The next night I was on the stage at St Johns leading praise and worship again. After service a PFLAG mother stopped me to say what a disgrace I was to the community and I should be ashamed of myself. One of my dearest friends was so very angry with me about letting the church down and letting God down as well. That was one of the best days of my life, for the first time I was letting the two worlds meet and I was very proud of who I was; and that I loved all of me. I looked at the mother and stated that I did that for me and I really didn't care how she felt about it. I thanked her for being a support for her son and that I needed to support myself and that is just what I had done. I asked my friend that day, who had best shown the face of love that day? Was it the folks who ask me not to march with the church group because of the way I was dressed, or was it me who being myself sharing my love with everyone from the songs I sang to riding with the local bar. I asked what Jesus would have done. I love that day because I had a breakthrough on many levels. I began to understand there was more to life than I had experienced. There was more to God than I had experienced. What about all these other faiths, what about all these cultures that had been around for decades longer than the one I was part of. I felt no shame for what I had done that day; I felt pride for the first time.

I was in the process of finding my true self and a path to loving the person inside for who I was. I had left so many of my vices behind years before. I had been clean and sober for over 10 years by this time and I knew I wanted more. More of life and a larger understanding of who God was and what God meant to me. I knew that I could never find it in North Carolina so I set out to see the world. I had friends in Australia who asked that I come for a visit and spend extended time with them. It was the greatest trip of my life.

For the first time ever I allowed my entire self to come out and play. I was pleased with my life. I had lost 50 pounds and joined the gym, I was changing my life. I loved all aspects of my life and I was determined to find a way to live my life for who I was no matter what anyone thought of me. Mardi Gras in Australia was just the place to start. I had the best tour guides ever. My friends Derrick and Warren showed me the trip of a lifetime. During the day we would sightsee and at night we would put on our leather and hit the town and have the time of our lives. I did things that surprised me yet I was not hiding who I was and I was not ashamed of it at all. I remember walking back to the hotel at 5 AM with my cod piece arriving at the hotel to call Derrick and Warren and asking them to bring me some clothes so I could get into the lobby.

Freedom for the first time in my life, and no one batted an eye and if they did, I didn't care. I had found peace with myself and I had found that there was so much more to life than living the life that everyone else wanted me to live. I wanted to live my life and be proud of who I was. I needed to find that person I had locked away inside of me and find a way to be me. I returned from that trip a very changed man. I knew I wanted to leave the south and see the world. I wanted to live on the west coast. I wanted to find out who I was to God and who God was to me. Within six months I traveled to Seattle WA, sold everything I had and shipped my art and cookware to Seattle. I moved in with someone I had only known for a couple weeks. When I arrived in Seattle it was very different than it had been in the south. Folks were not as friendly as in the south, yet they didn't really believe in the same way we did in the south either. I had wanted a change and that is just what I got. I was dating someone who didn't believe in God or anything really. I found a job and started excelling at it, I missed church as I knew it yet I knew I had to find myself. I would visit churches only to find them just like the ones on the east coast. It was the most segregated place on earth. Everyone holding onto what they knew was the truth about the other, no one willing to take the first step. Here I was this country boy from South Georgia, Alabama, and North Carolina going to visit an AME Zion church, singing my heart out. I finally met some friends, including one who wanted nothing to do with church, God, or anything religious. I was finding that I was agreeing on the religious part all too well. My other friend was all too willing to go and sit next to me, singing the whole way. I loved to be there singing, to have someone turn around to see who that was singing, and my friend Ritchard pointing his finger at me. I must have been asked 50 times where did you learn to sing that way. I know that I could have visited any church I wanted, I could have found the MCC in Seattle yet I wanted to live my life not based on the fact that I was a gay man, so I could find out who Allen was.

While living in the south I had always lived an open life, everyone knew I was a gay man and I was very happy with that fact. I was on my own at a very young age and learned that I wanted to be myself no matter what.

Chapter Four:

Old Habits

Here I was in the big city, I could be myself. I didn't need to fight for the rights of the other gay people in the world. I didn't hide who I was; I just wanted to know who I was without pushing against something, or someone because of my lifestyle. My business world was off the charts, and the company I was working for loved my work. I had presidents and vice presidents flying out to meet me and I was making more money than this country boy ever had seen. My southern charm was the ice breaker and I loved being from the south. I loved seeing mountains and oceans next to each other. I loved being in a city surrounded by water, I loved having a company car and not having to make a car payment. I loved having a minivan to haul everything I purchased around in. My romantic life however was at an all time low. I trusted someone again, and you guessed it, I had found a bad boy I wanted to change. (BS) Here is that belief system showing up again. I was changing. I was more confident in my work life than ever. I was not attending church yet I felt a connection to God that was more real than I had felt before. I was however still living my life from the belief system that I was... not good enough. The relationship ended and he moved away.

Some weeks later I had a visitor at my door telling me that, he and my ex-partner had been having a relationship on the side the entire time we had been dating. I listened, I took it in, I thanked him for sharing, and asked him to leave. I cried. I was mad. I moved all the furniture I had purchased from my ex in his move to the new city and put it in his storage locker. I called him and said there is no reason to call me back, your things are in storage and you can keep the money. I wasn't mad with either of them as much as I was with myself. I felt like a fool, a country bumpkin, what was I doing here playing in the big leagues? Who was I fooling? I didn't know how to play this game, and all the relationships I was finding myself in were proving that point, oh so well.

I was a bad guy magnet, it had to be them, it surely could not have been me. I threw myself into my work and stuffed the hurt down deep inside. I excelled at work and played as hard as I could on my off time. I wanted to learn the game of not being attached and having casual encounters as much as I could. For the next six months of my life I did both exceptionally well. I was at the top of my game at work. There was talk of promotion and moving me back to North Carolina and I knew I wanted no part of that. I had just got out of there. I had become the king of casual encounters at the sex clubs, and the bars. I had found a way to numb the pain of intimacy. Just don't have it at all. I stated to my friends I will never be in a relationship again. I was on the fast track to find out about the law of attraction, hidden beliefs, and belief systems (BS). Within a month I was moving to San Francisco to live in an open S and M relationship. I had told myself that since I couldn't trust anyone to be true, why tell a lie. Here was a way for me to give all my power to another person who said they would take care of me.

To say I was in over my head was an understatement. Here I was this boy from South Georgia in a city where when you walk down the street people stare at you and are so open about their sexuality I didn't know what to do. I had been making great money in Seattle but the cost of living in San Francisco was at the top of its peak and I was renting a room in the basement of a home with a 1/2 bath and going upstairs to shower and cook in a kitchen under renovation.

I was going out to the clubs, giving myself away to anyone and everyone, waking up on Monday and going to work and excelling. Talk about living in two different worlds. I cried everyday for the first year I was there, I was in a relationship I wasn't equipped to handle. I felt discarded, thrown away, used up, and wasted. Yet in my professional life I was on top of my game. I would numb out anytime I could with sex because I knew that if I ever touched drugs or alcohol again I would die for sure. It was early 2000 and I wasn't feeling well physically. There was "something inside of me" that told me to go and get tested for HIV.

I had made it through all of my life and all these relationships and managed to stay HIV negative and here I was, knowing in my core, I was about to get the news of my lifetime. I was alone, scared, numb, and afraid.

I took the test and waited the two weeks from hell and called for the news. The assistant stated I needed to come in and see the doctor. I thanked them for giving me my test results. The doctor called and asked me to come in; he needed to go over some things with me. I said I know I am positive and I need to be alone. I would come see him the next day. That was the loneliest day of my life. I was numb.

I went to the doctor and he told me about the advances in medicine and his suggestions. With the history of my friends and these medicines I chose to wait and see. I was mad at the world and everyone I had slept with since my arriving in California. I was mad at HIV for the countless lives it had taken. Was I to be the next? I was mad at the world for the ways it was showing up in my life. I was mad at God for allowing this to happen, so I chose to not feel at all. I chose to go on antidepressants for the next year and I was totally numb. I didn't feel anything, nothing, the pain was gone. I didn't' care about myself or how I looked. I was damaged goods and no one would ever want me again, anyway.

I didn't want to die this way. I didn't want to finish the dance this way. I remember the words of my friend Donald "I want you to get that you are lovable, and you are worth loving." Here was this guardian angel watching over me. I started to care for myself again. I did acupuncture, herbs, and I began to watch my diet, and started to exercise five days a week. I made a great friend and we decided to move into a flat together in the city. We both had healing work to do and it was a time of healing. I started painting my pain out. I started looking for a spiritual home that would love all of me. I started working harder than ever and my job showed it. The company I was working for at the time was going through a restructure and most of my work friends had been laid off. I was doing the work of 10 folks and it was taking a bite out of me. I needed to feel again so I asked to come off the antidepressant and within a week tears were pouring down my face and I knew I was in over my head.

The stress from my job was overwhelming. For the first time ever I had a boss who didn't like my work; or me! I was worried about being fired, being HIV positive, and having to move to Georgia to live with my parents as no one would ever want to love me again. It was time to take a trip home to Georgia and tell my parents that I was HIV positive. As I told them tears ran down their faces and they asked me who would take care of me once they were dead? I told them I had a community of friends who loved me very much and would take care of me. I did have some wonderful friends and yet I was so afraid of dying alone. I came home and threw myself back into my work, the job eased up a bit and I continued on the path I had been on. We had a company meeting within the next six months and while there I visited with my parents. While there I noticed, I had a boil on my hip above my butt cheek. It was very sore and I did everything I could to get it to open and relive the pain. Nothing worked. By the time I got back to California it had doubled in size and I was at the doctor's office.

I needed to get back to work as I had taken a few days for vacation time. The doctor looked at the boil and said I am calling the hospital you need to go in for surgery. You have a flesh eating staph infection. For the next two weeks I was in the hospital twice, had two surgeries to remove the staph infection. I was stressed, worried about losing my job, and knew that I needed to take care of myself. I stopped everything I was doing and I asked for help. I asked to be shown the community that would love me for who I was. I asked to be shown a space that was big enough for all the facets of God. And that I understand with clarity when I had found my new spiritual home.

Over the next three months my wounds were tended by my loving friend Michael. Michael would come and pick me up and drive me to his and Antonio's home and clean and dress my wounds. We would both cry through the process, me from the pain of the process and him for hurting me knowing it had to be done or back to the hospital I would go. I had always known that there was something greater than me throughout my life. Regardless of my path and what I was feeling I knew this to be true. During this process when I was feeling so very ugly, and not good enough, someone who had met me once before emailed to ask if I would be open to a visit. I explained that I was in recovery; he stated he was very open to visit all the same. At that moment I didn't know he was to be the angel to lead me to my spiritual home.

I was instantly attracted to him and wanted so much more than was ever possible and yet we had an amazing friendship and do to this day. Tim'm was open and honest about what he had to offer and we became great friends. I loved his poetry, music and became one of his greatest fans. We hung out and I had asked him if I could go to church with him sometime. He said "where I go is not really a church; it is so much more!" I was very intrigued. I let it go and our friendship continued. I supported his music, and poetry readings and our friendship grew. Tim'm would come by and stay at my place from time to time and I welcomed his company.

One Sunday morning we woke up early and he said get dressed, I asked where we were going and he said we are going to East Bay Church of Religious Science. I was so very excited and yet nervous all at the same time. It was the 10:00 am service. We walked in the building and it was packed, so packed we couldn't even sit together. I looked around the space and was taking it all in, when the choir was announced and they started to process. Music has always been one of those places in my heart where God speaks to me clearly. This was no exception; the Mass choir was singing the song "Taste and See." The flood gates began to open and they flooded over my face for the remainder of the service. The song was touching everyone present in the center in such a way, that the minister stood up and started talking "about tasting the goodness of God. Taste it and see. To see what God could do in your life and to realize that you and God were one and that God wanted you to have a life filled with good that you could indeed taste and see."

I was overcome with joy when I heard the words in my ear "Welcome home." I had never been a part of a community this size, and being from South Georgia, and North Carolina where we were blessed to have 300 on a good day, to be in a room filled to overflowing with more than 400 at this one service was a bit much for me to take in. When the service was over, Tim'm and I were standing out in front as the folks poured out to the main entrance. I remember saying to him, "you may never come back here again but I will be back next Sunday." It was the beginning of a journey to a relationship with God like I had never had before.

Each Sunday I would sit in this service filled to overflowing and listen to this amazing minister, Rev. E, tell her story knowing full well it was mine as well. Rev E. had been raised in rural South Florida on a farm. I felt and understood everything she said. It was like being back home, yet the message was very different. I was being asked to understand and believe that God and I were one, there was no place were God stopped and I started or where I stopped and God started. We were all part of the same "Stuff". This pushed me past anything I had ever heard before much less anything I had ever preached before. Each week I would come and listen and cry because for once in my life it was all making sense. I began to believe that it was possible for God to be my friend, my best friend, someone I could have a heart to heart talk with and not worry about being whacked on the head. Now that was a lot to put my head around. It was the first time in my life with all the churches, gatherings, interfaith services in my life where I felt everyone was welcome regardless of the belief, sexual preference, or ethnic makeup.

I was happy to ask all of my friends to come and be a part of this experience. I was starting to meet new folks and make new friends. I wanted to sing in the choir more than ever and would sing with all my heart in the service and have folks say "you should join the choir." I have been in some amazing choirs in my life and sang with symphonies and been soloist on stage in front of thousands and yet here I was saying, I am not good enough. I had been in gospel choirs and I had been in choirs that were diverse and yet there was that old BS (belief system) hitting me in the face again. "YOU ARE NOT GOOD ENOUGH TO SING WITH THEM"! To say that I am rhythmically challenged does not begin to describe it. When I was in the choir at St John's the director would put me in the middle and say "stand still and sing honey that is all I want you to do." I was scared to death to be asked to clap, sway, and sing all at the same time that was a comedy routine just waiting to happen. So I sat on the sidelines playing small one more time.

One Sunday Rev E. read a passage written by Marianne Williamson:

> "Our deepest fear is not that we are inadequate. Our deepest fear is that we are powerful beyond measure. It is our light, not our darkness that most frightens us. We ask ourselves, who am I to be brilliant, gorgeous, talented, fabulous? Actually, who are you not to be? You are a child of God. Your playing small does not serve the world. There is nothing enlightened about shrinking so that other people won't feel insecure around you. We are all meant to shine, as children do. We were born to make manifest the glory of God that is within us. It's not just in some of us; it's in everyone. And as we let our own light shine, we unconsciously give other people permission to do the same. As we are liberated from our own fear, our presence automatically liberates others."

When I heard this being read, I knew I had to ask about the choir and being a part of it. I remember asking Michelle Jordan about it after service and she looking at me with one of those "who is this southern white boy wanting to sing in the choir" looks. I talked to her about leading praise and worship, and being in various choirs, and that I was very scared to sing with them as it was new to me. I was very used to singing traditional gospel music and yet I knew this was what I wanted to do. She asked had I taken foundations yet. When I asked what is foundation, she stated it was a class that was required in order to sing with the choir. She asked me to come that week and sit in on a choir rehearsal and see what I thought. I walked in sat in the back of the room. It was very different from Sundays as the only folks in the building were the folks there to sing. I have always been an early bird so I was one of the first folks there and when Michelle arrived we starting talking about my history and more about my journey and we made a connection. She asked me to come up and sit with the choir and listen. I was delighted to hear they were singing a song from a gospel tradition that I knew and was very familiar with. Michelle asked various folks to sing a solo verse and she asked me to sing one. She looked at me and said "let's hear what you can do Georgia boy."

My toenails were shaking I was so nervous. Someone else started the song and I closed my eyes and I was in that place of sweetness where I knew it was just God and me and I opened my mouth and outcome the most beautiful sound I think I have ever heard. The choir went wild and Michele looked at me and asked me if I could sing with the choir on Sunday.

I had to enroll in foundation class that was starting the next month in order to sing in the choir and I had to complete it in order to keep singing. At that moment I would have done anything. I was doing one of the things I had come here to do, sing. One of the many things I loved about my time at East Bay was singing with the choir. Here I was singing with a choir like I had dreamed about all my life. I would listen to Mississippi Mass Choir and sing my heart out in the car and yet from the world I had been a part of, that would never happen. It was up there with gay folks can't be Christian.

Here I was in heaven and enjoying every moment of it. We finished rehearsal and Michelle asked what color are we wearing this Sunday? East Bay International Choir was known for wearing a different color each week so here I was in heaven again. I think the color was brown and orange that week and I was one of those folks that needed to look good. I asked one of the guys in the choir for a good place to shop and he told me about a place that was off the chain. I took down the information and that next week I walked into the store for the first time. It was a store just for men and it had every color under the rainbow and the best part was there were more men's shoes than I had ever seen in my entire life, EVER!!!! I was like it can't get any better than this. I found a new shirt, a new pair of shoes and joined the mailing list that day. When I came back the next week for the new color I walked in and they had a sale on shoes, buy one pair get one pair for a dollar. Within a few months I had well over one hundred pairs of shoes in every color and style you can imagine. It become the joke before long to see if Brother (that was my name now in the choir) could work this out. I loved the challenge and rose to the occasion well. This went on for weeks when someone suggested "roots" I had to ask what that meant and it was about wearing things from your heritage. I knew I was English and Scottish so I started looking online to find out more about my tartan and family information.

Here I was going back to the beginning of who I was and finding out more about myself and loving it. I found my tartan and ordered my first kilt ever. The next month was the start of foundation class and everyone from the choir told me I would love the class and my life would change forever. Michelle reminded me in order to stay in the choir I had to take and complete the class. It started the next Saturday at 9:00 am. I showed up for class with 50 other folks. We had about 15 men and the rest of the class was women. That didn't worry me; to be honest I had done better with women on the friendship level than men. Week after week I would dig and go deeper and with each class the numbers would go from 45, 40, 35, and finally down to 15 at the end.

I would learn from this something that serves me to this day. In order to build a spiritual life I needed a foundation and that is exactly what I built in that time. I found during this time that I could and would take the doors off of my understanding of God. Who I had believed God to be in my life, and with each expansion I would grow to call it "Divine." I learned for the first time that now included me. Each and every day I had a process and some days it was one step forward and 2 steps back. Yet the path was broader than it had ever been. I was loving my life, thriving in business, and financially I was making more money than I ever had. There was one aspect of my life that I knew needed to change and yet I was unwilling to let that aspect go. It was the one area of my life where I was the rebel and I would often state "I have given up alcohol and drugs. I'll be damned if I will give up sex!" So I kept that part hidden from my newfound friends or I would find friends who had the same understanding. I lived this life and I thought it was all going well. Little did I know there was a time bomb ticking away inside the cells of my body.

Chapter Five:

Rubber Meets the Road

"There are moments in our life that make us; that set the course of who we're gonna be. Sometimes they're little, subtle moments. Sometimes, they're not...Bottom line is, even if we see them coming, we're rarely ready for the big moments. Few of us ask for our life to change, but it does. So what does this make us? Helpless? Puppets? No. The big moments are going to come. We can't do anything about that. It's what we do afterwards that matters. That's when we find out who we are!" Jim The Daily Buddha

When I think back on when I received the news that I was HIV positive, I really lived in a state of numbness for years. It did, however, call me to a physical fitness level that I had never had before. I was in the best physical shape of my life working out 5 days a week, body fat in check, looking good and very active. I was living the good life. I was making more money than I ever had in my life. I was living in a luxury apartment in the bay area of California. I was surrounded by fine things and good people.

When I realized that I was feeling fatigued and needing to take naps which had never really been the case, I decided to go in and see the doctor about it. Being HIV positive and not on medication I remember all of my friends who had been positive before me and their experiences with the medications and refused to go on them until I had no choice. I was now at choice after the blood work and a follow up visit, as well as a long talk with my best friend. I agreed to go on HIV medication which was one of the hardest decisions I had made. As my body became accustomed to the medication the process was quite a journey. I took time off work to deal with the fatigue and new medication and within thirty days had developed a lump on my neck.

I went back to the doctor very angry and stated this is exactly why I didn't want to go on HIV medicine in the first place. He assured me that it would go down and that life would be back to normal in no time. I went home and for the first time ever I began to ask my body "what is going on in there"? Who knew our bodies would respond to us when we ask them what is going on. I certainly didn't. I felt this overwhelming fear, as if I were crazy talking to myself. I really felt my body saying to me this is more than the new medication please honor me and ask for more tests. A week later the lump had doubled in size and I made another appointment to see the doctor. He wanted to wait a month and see if the lump would go down, yet I kept hearing my body asking me to honor it and ask for more tests. For the first time in my life I honored myself and asked the doctor to send me to have a biopsy. He referred me to another wonderful doctor who agreed with him that it was the medication and nothing to worry about. They did agree to be on the safe side, and to honor my request to have a biopsy.

Tick, tick, tick.

It was as if the seconds were days and I had to keep reminding myself that it was all good. I found myself wanting to celebrate my life and remember the countless lives that had made it possible for me to get the HIV treatment I needed without the side effects and death.

Here is an article I had written for a cancer journal in 2006.

My current journey started in January of 2000, when I heard the doctor say Allen, you are HIV positive. I was not surprised at the news. Stating that doesn't make the news any easier to hear. One of the first thoughts that crossed my mind was, am I going to die? I then remember the friends that I have the honor of knowing, who had journeyed this path, and shared their stories that make my journey easier.

My doctor advised me of medical breakthroughs, and studies that show early HIV medical treatment would ensure a longer life span. I had to make a decision that was right for me. With regular blood work, and the fact that my T Cells where high and my viral load remained stable I made a choice to go into psychotherapy and not go on HIV medication. The key word is CHOICE! I want to speak about listening to your heart. As a result of psychotherapy I was able to step through my fear and tell my friends and family about my HIV status. In that process, there were those who chose to walk away. I know that had nothing to do with me.

Out of my sharing about my status with others it opened the door for others to talk to me about their journey and let me know of the hope that I gave them and the freedom to share with someone else. I would never wish anyone this process, however I am very happy that my journey has helped make someone else's easier.

One of the main reasons I did not want to go on medication was fear. Fear of side affects, quality of life, and to be honest, having to admit to myself that I really had HIV and Aids. One of the ways I combated this was to change the way I lived my life. I began to work out 3 to 5 days a week and monitored what I took into my body. I also began to seek other forms of treatment: herbs, acupuncture, and other natural medicines. I continued to seek advice and monitor my blood work with my doctor as well.

In August 2006, I began to feel very tired and had a lack of energy. I didn't really understand this as I was working out 5 days a week and was taking great care of myself. What was going on and why was I feeling so tired? After going to the doctor with flu like symptoms and fatigue month after month, we checked my blood again, and we found that my liver panel was elevated. Once again I was at the place where I had to make a decision that was best for me. Was it time to start the medicine and overcome my fears?

I called my two greatest friends and asked them what they thought. They both advised me to go on medicine, so in November 2006, I started HIV medication. Everyone has their own journey with new medication and I had been told by my doctor within a month I should feel like my old self again.

I decided that a trip would do me good. Off I go to visit one of my dearest friends. While there I noticed a growth on my neck... Now what?

I made an appointment with my doctor who felt it was the lymph nodes reacting to the medicine and it would go down in a couple months and all would be well. I didn't agree! The swelling and the pain was increasing each day. I asked for more tests.

A CT scan revealed several enlarged lymph nodes. I was then referred to a throat specialist. He assured me by stating he was 95% sure that this was not CANCER but a cyst. He wanted to get a biopsy to make sure however. While at the biopsy I had a strange feeling... the same feeling I had when I was told I was HIV positive.

Two days later I get a call from my doctor asking me to come in for a talk. I was told that I had Lymphoma and I needed to see an oncologist immediately. The oncologist needed a tissue sample which meant I had to have surgery. Here is the GREAT NEWS, in all of this I knew this wasn't my last dance. I knew there was a Divine plan and I was on the journey of my life. Having this attitude has been the best medicine yet. Every time I had any blood drawn I looked for the Divine and goodness. Every time I would go for chemotherapy I called it LOVE JUICE. I visualize the IV fluid flowing in my veins as the love of the

Divine. Every scan, every procedure I had I looked for the good in it.... and good shows up every time! This is the attitude I have chosen to keep with me the rest of my life. If you take only one thing from my journey take this. I CHOOSE TO SEE GOOD IN EVERYTHING!!!!!! In the following pages you will find my journey into JOY.

With Great Love Allen Mosley

"Our struggles make us seek enlightenment from those around us and the stars above. However, it is when we uncover the light within that we finally illuminate a path once enshrouded by our false sense of incompleteness." —Dodinsky

Chapter Six:

The Journey to Joy

The preceding chapters are what I called the "Namaste Experiences." These are the original writings of when I blogged about my daily journey with cancer. Each day I would look deeper for the good in each experience with the knowing that it would indeed show up as Divine. With this tiny shift, I began to see the good in every situation, thought, outlook, procedure, and every needle. I saw the good everywhere because I wanted to see it.

December 01, 2006

Well the news came in today the biopsy showed that Lymphoma is present in the growth on my neck. Wow I am so glad that I was so persistent about getting this checked out. FEAR did happen today. Oh my God. Then I remember the words that had been said to me "you are not alone and I have this, just be prepared for the journey".

So I asked the doctor what was next, he gave me the name of the oncologist that I am to see and told me not to be afraid. In that moment I will have to say I think I was more numb that anything. I was just thinking about being prepared. I know such a Virgo right? I knew in that moment that it was important to start laughing; in the famous words of Rev E "TAINT SO!!!" I began to think about the humor in it all, here it was World Aids Day and I find out that Lymphoma is present in some of my cells. So rather than go to the Concert and hear what we so often hear about the DEADLY disease of AIDS, I decided to come home and spend some time with The Divine, have a pizza, and think about what was meant by being prepared.

I made sure all my bills were on my online banking bill pay so that I or anyone could go on there and pay them. My home was organized and was clear of clutter. I had pictures around me of all the loved ones in my life. For this is the place I would be on this journey so I wanted to make sure I felt LOVED and could see it happening. I had Beautiful pictures of me Radiating Perfect Health. As a matter of fact, I had taken some pictures earlier that day in some new leather clothes I had purchased and the Santa Hat that David had made for me. No matter what, I knew the outcome, that I am a Radiant Healthy Loving Divine Being.

Love Allen

In thinking back I began to look at who was in my life, what I was looking at, and what I was reading. I asked every friend I had at East Bay Church of Religious Science what books I should be reading. I wanted to take in and know my truth regardless of what the doctors and other folks said. I began to love myself in a new way and I knew what I needed to hear and what I didn't. I realized for the first time that I wasn't responsible for anyone else's happiness except mine and if my friends needed to cry or grieve, they needed to do it while not around me. I began to fill my life with LOVE, LOVE, and more LOVE! I didn't think about "How did this happen?" I started reading. What I knew from my foundation class was some part of me had drawn this in and I had two choices. I could continue on this path and die, or I could decide where I want to go from here and focus on that until it manifested. I chose the latter. I found that everything about who I had been before was expanding, changing, and growing. I was looking at life from this new perspective and choosing for myself what I wanted next. I began to look at what "God" was to me, how to have a relationship with who God was in my life. At times, I had been very afraid of God and yet knowing that I was one with the greater I AM. I began to realize my voice was important and in order for me to have what I wanted, I had to ASK, speak my own truth, believe, and "Know that it was so." I became my own practitioner, healer, truth speaker, and understood that it was there all along under all the grief, shame, not good enough, that was cluttering up my life.

Blog Day two (Asking for what I need) December 02, 2006

Hello my wonderful family;

I know that all of you have been awaiting the news from the biopsy, and it is finally in. I talked with the doctor yesterday and the biopsy shows that I have lymphoma. Now I want to start this off by saying don't worry and don't feel sorry for me. What I want from my family is LOVE and I know that I have that from each and every one of you. I called a lot of you yesterday to tell you and some I couldn't get through to so I wanted to make sure you all knew.

What I want from each of you right now, and throughout this journey is to hold me in PERFECT HEALTH. I will be saying that to myself on a daily basis as needed. I need the same from you. There is greatness in this. For I know that anything that happens in my life is for my good.

Here is what I know so far. I have a meeting with the oncologist on Tuesday around 3:00 PM, and then I will know more. I will have to have a full body CT scan; you all know how much I love that. It is actually not bad, I feel like the filling in a donut. I know crazy right? They will also at some point take a bone marrow biopsy on me as well. I will be at the gym 5 days a week and doing what I can to keep my body strong and healthy. They tell me that is very important. They suggest keeping your routine. Anybody up for 4:30 AM workouts let me know. Ha ha ha!

The one thing I do know is there is ministry in this, and I am choosing to walk this path. I don't know where all it is going to take me but I am ready, for I have the love of the Divine and all of you to see me through it all. I want you all to picture with me what joy that I am going to have telling everyone about this once it is all finished. Wow, now that is amazing.

I am covered at work for the next couple of months, and I will find out more as we see where this all goes. The doctor did tell me that we caught this early due to the fact that I was so very persistent about finding out what was going on in there. He also stated that he doesn't think I will ever have to go into the hospital; I can do this all as outpatient and be home in my own bed.

THANK YOU!!!

My friend Shawn is going to take me out today to have some fun and shop. I want to play this weekend. It is a great day to be alive and I am living it up. I am thinking about going to the city tomorrow and see if I can find a dance. And you all know where to find me tomorrow during the day I will be at the East Bay Church of Religious Science getting my full Praise on.

I am going to attach a picture of me taken yesterday so you all know how healthy I am and full of life. Please don't be sad, live with me and love with me. Know that I have chosen this path for the greater expansion and the knowingness of what is on the other side. I can't wait to tell my story. You know it is going to be a good one and all of you are going to be in it. Who knows they may even make a movie out of it. SMILE.

Please know that I love you all and treasure you with every breath I take.

All my love Allen

I love reading this blog, it really reminds me of the Joy I was living right then, or as I like to refer to it, the Joy of now. I had just been told I had one of the most aggressive cancers there is and I chose to be happy about it. I was happy, I was free to love and live. I had just been given the key to the cell door and I was out of the prison that I had placed myself in for years. In that moment I realized that life was for living, and I wanted to live it. In an instant I wanted to call everyone I knew and tell them I loved them. I let go of everything that I had been holding on to; resentment, grief, anger, disease... what I know today is I had allowed my life to consume me literally and figuratively, from the inside out. Now was the time to change all that, if this was indeed my final dance I wanted it to be the dance of my life. I wanted to be remembered for being love, not hate, resentment, or being a victim.

I called everyone I had any hard feelings toward and made amends. It didn't matter who I felt was at blame, I wanted to love with everything within me. I was remembering who I was and why I came here in the first place. I was building a relationship with my body, my soul skin and I was listening to it like I never had. With each phone call, email, and letter, I became more free. With each I Love You I said to my friends and family, I become more and more free. I was living the Joyous life I had been calling in. I was living this life without concern for what was next because I knew that I had the magic key. I had control of how I choose to see things and I was responsible for my happiness regardless of appearances.

December 02, 2006

I woke up this morning at 4 AM, my usual time to go to the gym. I had a good cry to let out some of the emotion. Then, I said to myself, it is time to go to the gym; staying healthy and strong is very important. This is true whether you are on a medical journey or just day-to-day life. I realized one of the reasons that the doctors didn't see the possibility of lymphoma was due to the fact I am so very healthy, and strong. I had a great workout, came home, and, here is the humor; I had the last 3 slices of pizza from the night before. I took the time to write all of my friends that I was unable to reach the night before and emailed them about my journey with the Divine. I called and checked in with my parents and told them how happy I was and that I was the perfect person to go through this as I love to talk, so telling the good news would be easy. I wanted them to know that deep in my heart I wasn't scared. I was relieved in a way just to know the truth so I could get started on the healing journey.

I called a friend and asked him to go shopping and have some fun. Within the hour, we were shopping, having fun and enjoying each other's company. I strongly recommend this. Being with him helped my wandering mind. By five that evening I was ready for an evening at home alone. I watched a little TV, sent out an email to the choir, and got my clothes ready for Church the next day. It was very important that I look fabulous. I wanted the world to see that my insides and my outward appearance were shining brightly. I must say I looked great, red and black head to toe and one of my favorite pairs of shoes as well. Can't beat that! Off to bed ready for an early day at church the next day.

I love you Allen

One of the greatest gifts I got out of this journey was learning to "Ask for what I needed." I had started reading Ask and It is Given by Ester and Jerry Hicks, I strongly recommend all their books. I also re-read Louise Hay's You Can Heal Your Life over and over again. It really didn't matter why I was here; I knew consciously where I wanted to go and how I wanted to live the remainder of my life. If there was going to be a change it was up to me. So rather than asking "WHY" I began to ask what are you here to teach me? I begin to ask for the courage to look at what was coming up and to honor my body for the first time ever. For most of my life I used my body as a tool to get what I wanted, or to give it away to someone else for pleasure. For the first time ever I was in a relationship with my body to honor it and ask for what it needed. It was the beginning of the journey to a new life and I loved how it felt. I was building a relationship based on trust, and if I needed to rest, I rested. If I needed to play I would find a friend, who would go shopping, to the park, sit at the ocean, and play. Asking for what you need is the greatest gift you give yourself and you set others free to do the same.

December 03, 2006

Got up this morning checked my email and got some amazing emails from some of my friends. The love is so amazing and I feel so very blessed to have the honor of being in each of their lives. Took my morning meds and off to church I go. What a loving family I have at East Bay. I am so blessed that the Divine led me to this place to find family. I have been to some amazing churches in my life. Been touched and felt the love of God in all of them. St Johns MCC was one of the churches where I felt the most love and to be honest the most spiritual growth. After moving from NC I felt that I would not find that again. So I searched only to find that I was making that statement true. So I asked once again while living on MacArthur Blvd in Oakland to show me home!!!! One Sunday, one of my friends who I had the most amazing CRUSH on, got up and said let's go to church. I had asked him before about his church and told him that I would like to go with him one day. I cried the entire service with joy for I knew at that moment I was home. I have been back almost every Sunday since. This Sunday I was greeted with love and support as always and some of the Choir had read my email and thanked me for my honesty and truth. I was bathed in love and family. I went to the second service as well where I had the honor to sit with Bishop. One of the many friends I have in my circle called family. He didn't miss a beat and was not sad, which I had asked for. He asked me how my play day was and what did I buy? What a great man and friend I have in Bishop. After church I was greeted by friends and then off to meet Shawn to have lunch and play again. We decided to meet later that day, so I went in to the city to visit my friend David and help him with a project he was working on. Later Shawn and I had dinner and a great visit, then off to bed to hit the gym the next day.

I love you Allen

Surrounding myself with folks that would hold me in perfect health was one of the greatest gifts I had in this process. My family and I had not been close for some time and I had created this new family, a family of choice and these were the folks I wanted to take this journey with. They had been there to celebrate the good times and I knew they would be there to celebrate the even better times I was about to embark on. Choosing who I hung out with was the beginning of a lifelong lesson, take a look around and see who are the 5 people you spend the most time with. Ask yourself these questions?

Are they living the life I want to live?

Are they loving the way I want to love?

Are they living their purpose?

Are they people I would give the keys to my home to?

These where questions I needed to ask myself, and as Rev. E would say "Honey sometimes you have to look at the expiration date and make sure they are still good for you!" I loved my family with all I have and yet I knew that I needed folks on my path that would hold me at my highest and best. I needed to be with my family of choice, this was my journey and I was responsible for asking for what I needed and loving myself.

December 04, 2006

Got up and went to the gym. It was a struggle as I just wanted to stay in bed. I reminded myself that as I was on this journey I may feel that way from time to time, so it was important to make myself go. I didn't want to ever give in or up to TAINT SO (cancer). Part of this whole journey was to have fun and laugh at this. So off to the gym I went, came home and prepared all the things I needed to do that day. I find it important to make a list so I can check it off and stay up to date each day. I did banking, errands and met with David.

Got a call from Dr. Rust, he is the doctor that ordered the biopsy. He wanted to meet with me and talk. I also had a meeting with Dr. McGraw that day as well. I felt so much love from both of them and they wanted me to know that they were there for me. Got all the paperwork and my list was complete. I came home to have a nice evening at home for tomorrow will be the first meeting with the oncologist. Off to bed.

I love you Allen

December 05, 2006

Family,

Wanted to keep you all up to date on where we are in this trust walk I am taking with the Divine. I met with the oncologist yesterday, Dr. Knopf (don't even ask me to try and say it.) I am calling him a very nice man. He ordered blood work which I did yesterday, one down. They will remove the gland in my neck as they need that to see just what type of lymphoma that I have. (Over 50 types, fast, slow, B, T cell, etc.) They will take the gland and section it off to see what the best form of treatment is. The Sergeant is a wonderful man that helped me with the biopsy. I will have about a 4-hour surgery due to the gland being involved with the SPECIAL gland that I don't have a clue how to spell. This gland is responsible for the facial muscles and any damage to it can leave me as the doctor puts it looking like Betty Davis after the stroke. I was hoping to have the surgery this week, but due to the nature of the procedure it has to wait until the week of the 20th. BREATHE!!!

This Friday I have a full body CT scan, they will be looking to see if the lymphoma is in the other lymph glands as well. This is to stage the growth and lets them know how fast it is growing and how much Love Juice to give me. As it looks now I should have my first chemotherapy before Christmas. Talk about new birth in the New Year, my bottom will be as smooth as it was when I was born. (No Hair) Just for the record that is a lot of hair, the humor in this is that I know that Spirit knows how many hairs are on our bodies, and I think maybe the Angel in charge of my count needed a little vacation. (This is the part where we all laugh.) I have a great deal of hair, part of my family tree.

Next Friday on the 15th I will have a bone marrow biopsy; this is to see if the lymphoma is in my bone tissue. I know that this is not the case, but they still need to test so they can see what I already know.

Once the doctor has the gland tissue and the CT Scan then we will know how long I will be on chemo as well as how often I will have to have chemo. Yesterday was a great day and I really love the doctors that I have. I am a very blessed man to have all this Love washing over me and through me. Just like I learned from my faith walk in Foundation, I am learning so much about how I handle things, and how the Divine is showing up in my life. I am not scared and I am ready for the next step in this walk. For I know that each step is Divinely Guided.

I love you all Allen

December 06, 2006

Family,

Funny how that word means so many different things. For the longest time in my life it brought pain, because my family could not love me for who I am, however my truth stood the test of time, and you are my witness to that. Having my Mom, and Dad visit the East Bay Church last August, hearing how they loved it healed us. In contrast there is growth. Thank you.

For a great deal of my life I looked for the Magic Pill, I looked in drugs, alcohol, sex, food...etc. My truth stood out, and let me know the magic pill is ME. It is my attitude, how I choose to look at things. How I choose to react to things. How I choose to take care of myself. I have now been in recovery from alcohol, and drugs for over 20 years. What a journey in learning to love self in a new way. At church last night the choir circled around me in Love and Light -- a Love ring. One that I can choose to take off at any time, or I can choose to hold that love close to me and treasure family. Thank you, Divine family.

In the words of Rev E, "TAINT SO," about the cancer, taint so about what is showing up in my life right now. I know my truth, and with each of you I hold myself in perfect health. I know the truth, and I know how Divine Law works, so it has no other way but to show up. And so it is.

Thank you all for the inspiration, love, joy, laughter, and the hugs! Those are the best, keep them coming please. Thank you for the opportunity to love, and live out loud. This is growth.

I love you Allen

December 07, 2006

I spent time with Avery, James and Mag Pie today, so good to see them again. We rode the cable car to Pier 39 to see the sea lions and visit. Then I was off to the eye doctor for a visit, he placed me at risk for glaucoma. He stated that I have a tear in my eye as well, most likely an accident or hard knock to the head. I guess that means I need to pad the head board. I am so funny I make myself laugh. Humor is one of the greatest healers there is. I realized that I love to laugh and learning to laugh at myself is one of the greatest gifts. Let's just say that when you look up A-type personalities, there is a picture of me right there. The joy of humor is letting go of the attachment of control and allowing the joy of the journey to be just that "the journey, not the destination."

I find that humor is really the best thing. I learned to laugh and to have fun along the way. So many times I would sit next to someone in the clinic and hear the words "fight the disease" or I will not give up without a fight. Today I know that what I found served me best in the process was to surrender, (not lie down and die) just to surrender to the process. I knew that anything I push against pushes back, and it was my intention to have a joyous experience on this journey. I didn't want to fight cancer, I wanted every cell in my body to remember who it was and why it came here in the first place, and surrender was the best path for me. Fighting meant that I was choosing to struggle in the process and I didn't want that in my life. I had been living that life all of my life and that is what got me to this space. I wanted something new. For me that required surrender.

I love you Allen

December 08, 2006

Full day

Dentist visit. I will have some work done first of next year once Dr Eslao speaks with Dr. Knopf. I will need to pick up some teeth trays to make sure I have fluoride on my teeth when I am having the chemo treatments.

Off to the doctor's office to get the lab work for the blood draw. Had the blood work drawn by a great tech that was able to get the vein right away and it didn't hurt. She was really cool. She had a low sexy voice when she was focused. It was fun talking with her.

Off to get the drink for the CT scan, I was reminded how wonderful it is to be able to drink and eat at will. By the time I had the CT scan I was ready to drink DIRT. I talked to mom and told her the barium was actually really good, funny what happens when we shift our consciousness.

Off to see Dr. McGraw. Showed him the new lumps in my neck and told him that I had an eye exam the night before. He wanted more blood work to check the CD4 and Viral Loads.

Off to the CT scan. I met with Frank, who set up the "IV" and got me ready for the CT scan. He is really nice and told me that I looked like I was in great shape and good luck with the treatments and that he would see me soon for another scan to check the progress. After a day filled with appointments I was ready to rest and recharge myself. Learning to honor my body is a journey and serves me well.

I love you Allen

December 09, 2006

Tomorrow I go and visit my folks and I am really excited to see them. I really want to spend some time with my dad and make sure he knows how much I love him. He has been having a really hard time with all of this. I am reminded that choice has a great deal to do with how I look at things in the world. Yesterday was a full day of treatments, from the blood draw, dentist, doctor visits, and CT scan. I was reminded when I look for the face of the Divine that it shows up. Thank you.

Avery, James and Mag Pie are here for a visit so I get to show them around today and visit with them before they go back to LA. It has been so good to see them. They are coming over this morning and I am going to give them one of my paintings. I want them to have a piece of who I am.

I found a couple more lumps in my abnormal area, I just know that means that the "Taint SO" is growing and will be treated with great haste. I am very grateful this part of the journey will begin soon. I have been feeling a bit tired and get a bit fatigued after a day out, but I am resting when I need to and going on with my day's activities.

I got up this morning and cleaned up the house a bit before my travel I am looking forward to the trip I get to see my nephew and his family tomorrow night.

I feel really good today, and it is a great day to be alive.

Thank you. Allen

It was at this time I created a journal that I carried with me everywhere I went. Before I would go in to an appointment I would set my intention, one of the many take aways from Ester and Jerry's books. I would write what I wanted the outcome to be and I would say it to myself over and over again and then read it again before going to the appointment, procedure, doctor visit, phone call, etc. The setting of intentions serves me to this day; it is my way of asking the universe and aligning with my truth. I don't really need to know how it works just that it does work.

December 10 -14, 2006

Trip to visit my family. It is funny to see how my vision and the Divine's sometime show up different. My nephew picked me up from the airport and the next day I had a chance to meet my great niece and nephew for the first time. What great children, and Jimmy's wife is a very nice woman as well. We talked about ways to change their home and work with the things they have. I love helping my family and friends.

Mom and dad picked me up on the 11th and we drove back to Georgia. I am so very blessed to have my parents. Funny how I had hoped that my letter to my Dad would arrive before I did, there was a much bigger and better plan. My Dad got the letter the day I arrived. I would never have thought I would enjoy watching him read the letter from me; however I must say it was a real treat. One thing I had to let go of is what I needed (attachment) and let it be just what it was. Seeing his face and knowing that he will keep it and read it from time to time will be something that will stay with me forever. Lesson learned, relax and enjoy the journey.

My family and I went out to eat on the 12th and it was so funny to see how different we are. I can talk to a rail, as my Mama would say, and my brother Glenn is this quiet gentle man. My sister is this light of love. I look at us sometimes and I think where did I come from. So very different, my brother lives about 10 minutes from my mom and my sister about 15. I, on the other hand, live on the other side of the country. They have family in the traditional sense and I have family of choice. Both equally blessed and all our needs met. Thank you. My Dad took me to see my Aunt Judy, one of my all time favorite Aunt's while I was growing up. She was the song leader at Church when I was a young boy and I loved to hear her sing. So good to see her and know that she is happy.

On the 13th my Aunt Dovie came out for a visit. It is so good to see the love my dad has for his brother and sister. They are so very close and of course my dad takes care of them all. Such a strong quiet man, my brother is more like him day by day. My dad's mom was this strong amazing woman, and I really wish I could have known her in the flesh growing up. Every day I got to see who she was in the form of my Dad- hard working, strong, and always pushing us to do our best. Today I know that he was also loving. My niece Mareen and my sister in law came over to show me my niece's art work from school and she gave me one of her paintings. This journey keeps showing up as abundance every day. I love that and so much more.

On the 14th my dad, mom and my sister drove me to the airport to catch my flight home. Arrived home and took the shuttle. It was so very nice to be back in my apartment. I love my apartment and I am so blessed to have this as my home. What a great visit, and the knowledge that family comes in so many forms.

I am blessed. Allen

December 15 - 23, 2006

After arriving home I took some time to rest and ready myself for my upcoming surgery. I took the time to write in my journal and set my intention. It was my intention to see the Divine in every aspect of the process from the drive in, the person who checked me in, the nurses, and the doctor. I thanked everyone for being there and asked them to say nice things during the process and be kind to each other. I thanked Dr. Rust once more for being the hands of the Divine and doing a great job. It was my intention to sing the following Sunday and enjoy my visit with Richard. My intention was to have full use of my face and speak and sing with ease and grace. I kept repeating that to myself until I dropped off to sleep from the medicine.

Four plus hours later I woke up to more Divine faces and I spoke with ease and they asked me would I like something to drink and eat. I was so happy to see food; I said I would eat cardboard right now. We all had a great laugh and they called my ride home. I arrived home and checked in with my friends Antonio and Michael. They asked who was staying with me. I said I was great and going to go to bed. They stated they would be right over; I was going to stay with them that night.

Richard arrived the next morning and we had a great visit. I was sore but no pain. Richard and I watched movies and he cooked for me. He is a great cook. All of my intentions were manifesting and I was so excited to see them in action. It was the beginning of a journey with intentions that serves me to the present day.

December 24, 2006

Christmas Eve; what a great day to be alive! I woke up this morning grateful that I am alive and get to sing today. All of my Scottish clothes came yesterday; right on time! It is funny how I had released the need to control when they arrived. Surprise, surprise I have my kilt jacket. Fits like a glove. Thank you.

Got up. Richard is still asleep so I took my medicine, vitamins and started pressing my clothes. My neck is sore and tender. Four days after surgery I am up getting ready to go and sing. That is Divine action. I am Divine action today. I look great and feel great. I have my family with me; from the ring on my hand, to the clothes I am wearing, I have my history with me.

I get to church; one of the first there and Tyrone is so happy to see me. Bobby is so happy to see me. Everyone is so happy to see me. Gift shared a card from the choir, and the gift of being a gift.

We stand to sing and out comes the music. It is great! I am so excited that I am singing today. Why? Just because I can, it is an honor, a blessing, a sign of my faith in the Divine plan.

Richard is here, Shawn has been around, and Antonio and Michael have been around. I feel and see the Divine everywhere I go. One of the Choir members didn't know about the Taint So and started to hug me and I had to say we have to be careful I had surgery. What kind? I told them and then they didn't want to hug me. For the first time in my life, I got that wasn't my journey or my truth.

Thank you.

What a blessing to know in the moment someone else's journey isn't my journey. Rev E and Andrette were on today in church. I am so happy for being able to celebrate with them one more day.

I love you

Allen

There were times when I needed to share a personal journal entry just for me. Something I wanted to let go of and didn't want to share with the world. I was so happy to share my journey as I wanted to have my own truth about cancer and give others a chance to see it in a new light --, the courage to make their own choices, and have their own truth.

Personal Note to Self

Christmas Eve and it is time to go to church. I am so happy that Richard got here last night. I was a bit tired when he arrived, I went to bed and got some rest. My neck is sore a bit, it is swollen and a bit stiff. I am just so happy to be up and around after the surgery. I am going to sing at a couple of services and then come home and spend time with Richard. I can't wait to sing with the choir today. You know one of the things I have noticed the most in this process is just to relax, and everything works out for my highest and best; Amazing. Thank you.

Thank you for Perfect Health, Abundance, Love, Friendship, Joy and so much more.

I release and let go. And so it is.

December 25, 2006

Merry Christmas.

What a great day to be alive. Thank you for getting me up this morning and having the use of my body and joints. Thank you for Richard and his visit, and just letting him be here with me. It is great.

I got up and called Lori to sing her Happy B day. Ernest called me. He is always there and always so loyal. I love you Ernest J. Grant.

Called my Mom and Dad; so good to hear their voices as well. I am such a blessed man, I still have my parents and they are still together.

Waiting for Richard to get up so we can talk about what we are going to do today. Thank you for being here my friend. I love you.

What a great day to be alive.

Thank you.

I love you Allen

December 31, 2006

Good Morning

The last couple days I have been in a place that I thought was sadness. I couldn't quite put my finger on it. I feel so blessed and happy. I have been really thinking a great deal about my friendships. The not knowing what was going on with one of my friends who choose to step out of my life for a moment was weighing heavy on my mind. Not so much their actions, but instead asking where does this show up in my life? I thought about the times I had done the same. I was really hurt that my friend took themselves away from me, but then I thought about the fact that I too have done this. I began to focus more on their needs than mine. This was not an easy task, but I am grateful today all the same. Thank you for the growth. Last night when I was on the way to the choir party, I took the time to call my friend and tell him that I loved him.

I don't understand why I chose to feel separation when I know that there is only one life. When I stepped into that realization the hurt vanished. I could just love my friend no matter how it looked right now. I also realized it was FEAR. Fear that I couldn't count on him. Fear of being alone and in need, once again I felt the hands of the Divine and know that I am NEVER alone.

I have been clearing out my closets and my home of things that no longer serve me. I have abundance. Thank you for the reading in Science of Mind magazine. What a great life lesson.

I love you Allen

The journey was about to begin and I had one of my best friends coming in from NC who I totally trusted with my life. It is funny how everyone wants to tell you their chemo story or their cancer story in this time. It's funny really how we as folks think we are standing with our friends when in fact we are letting go of our fears around the process. I heard some real stories and then I woke up and said to all the folks around me, I DON'T WANT TO HEAR THIS, I want to have my own journey and I have called the folks in that I want to stand with me. If you don't want to laugh and joke with me please stay home. I want to laugh and have as much fun as I can.

Everyone has their own journey and I encourage you to find yours. Do you and your body a favor and make it as much fun as you can. The more I laughed at my life and myself for being so 'Type-A Virgo male,' the better it got. I realized that I was so serious about everything, and I do mean everything.

I was being gifted with the chance to see with a new pair of glasses and I wanted to enjoy them. You know those big sunglasses you get in the novelty store that are like 3 times the size of your head, those are the glasses I choose to see life through. I tell myself all the time that I am one funny man. I learned to laugh at myself and the many times that I saw only one way to do things well I had a million of them. Making the bed, washing clothes, vacuuming the rugs, washing the dishes, folding the clothes... I was finally finding the way to freedom and it came in the form of cancer, who knew?

I found that I wanted to spend as much time loving as I had been judging myself and others. Here I was getting ready for the journey of my life and I was laughing and making jokes all the time. I would laugh at myself and tell the funny stories about how funny I was. I was one of those folks that got dressed up to go to the gym; you never know who you might meet at the gym. You know Prince Charming goes to my gym! When I went to work I was decked out from head to toe, and I mean head to toe. The shirt matched the shoes and the socks matched the shirt and I had it going on. It was more important to "look good" than feel good. I had been living my whole life up to this point based on "looking good."

Now that was funny as heck. Here I was getting ready for my colon check up and if you have never had one of those let me be the first to tell you "IT AIN'T PRETTY AT ALL!" I couldn't get 2 feet from the bathroom or I would poo on myself, I am laughing just thinking about how funny that is. I went in the next morning with Ern and I was in sweats, an old t-shirt and slippers. I was free. Here you are with a gown open in the back with a TV monitor in front of you and the doctor asking, "Do you want to see?" Might I add passing gas the whole time, talk about your Virgo nightmare, now that was funny. I sat there smiling, thinking about all the times I had been so serious and buttoned up, closed off, looking good, and now finding great humor passing gas and laughing at myself. What a journey: I love it!

January 12, 2007

I thought I would check in to talk about the last week of events. Ern arrived on Sunday of last week and it is so good to have him here. I have felt so safe knowing he is here to go to chemotherapy with me.

We went out Sunday and had a fun day shopping, I took him to all my favorite spots and we got some cool things. On Monday, I had to do the prep for the colon check which showed that I was in great shape there and no need for another checkup for 5 years. I think the best news is in not having to do the prep for another 5 years. Now that is GOOD NEWS. I have some amazing friends and I am so happy that I have Ern here at this step in the journey. I really suggest that you get your best bro to be there on your first chemo day, you know the one that finds humor in everything and helps you not be so YOU (serious) about everything. Over the last year I have really looked at the love and friendship I have in my life. Thank you Spirit for all the great friends that bring such joy and love into my life.

Tuesday was the Colon day and then Ernest, Shawn and I had dinner together, which was really great. We had grits, shrimp and salmon patties. Nothing like those Southern friends to feed you great food. Thank you, Ern.

Wednesday got up and had a big breakfast before heading off to chemotherapy. The first day was a bit full and I really do recommend doing it all in one day. Blood draw first to check my blood count. Meeting with Dr. Knopf. Then chemotherapy time, it took six to eight hours to load all the medicine (love juice.) I had this Divine mantra I kept saying. I allow the love of the

Divine in. I kept looking at the bag of IV fluid and saying that over and over again. It really helps. I really recommend that you have a saying to keep your mind focused on the good. It really makes a difference in the process. After the chemotherapy was all done we had to go and pick up my medicine from the pharmacy. I was a bit tired by this point and was a bit cranky. We got it all done, got home in time to have a good meal.

I have been taking my anti nausea medicine and doing well. I feel a bit queasy from time to time but they say to stay ahead of the game: I would agree.

Ern and I went out today and I have to be honest; it was a bit much. I had a great time, really want to honor the body. Rest is the key and getting lots of liquids.

That is about it for today.

I love you Allen

Over the next few weeks I was really grateful for all the time I had taken before this process started. I was so pleased that all my bills were set up and I had put my home in order. It was in this process that I knew that I could not stay in my current space as my income was going to change in this process. I think of all the things that happened during the journey that was the thing that affected me the most. I loved where I lived and looking back I loved the way I looked living there. No judgment, I spent a great deal of time making the outside look good and I had not dealt with the inside in a long time. I didn't know what to do really so I called my folks to come and help me pack my apartment and put it in storage. My folks were super heroes and it was on this journey that I met my Dad for the first time in my life. I had known my Dad all along, and I had always wanted to hear the words I am proud of you and I love having you as my son. Here I was with no hair, bloated from the chemo, and packing all my belongings in a big box. That is when my Dad holds my hand and tells me how much he loves me and how proud he was of me and the journey I was on. He told me how he didn't think he could do it. He told me he loved how I was happy and joyous in the process. I had waited all my life to hear these words and they were really wonderful, the truth is I realized at that moment I loved myself for the first time and I liked how it felt. I loved who I was on this journey and I was proud of myself.

February 01, 2007

Hello Family

I think all of you know I have been spending the last month packing up with the help of my parents and friends. I wanted to talk to you about all the wonderful things that have been showing up for me. When I moved from the East Coast in 98, I moved with a few dishes (you know how I love my Calphalon), and my art work. One of the things I am realizing as I watched the boxes flow into the moving crate is the abundance in my life. One of the things you learn in early recovery is remember where you come from. "But for the grace of God there go I."

When I first heard about the cancer my only thought was what to do next? I knew in my heart that there is a Divine plan and it was up to me just to watch it all come together. When I heard about my pay coming to an end, again I just knew that it'll all work out. In the past when life happened I was so angry. One of the things I was sharing with my Mom today is I asked Spirit this last year to be debt free. I know that I am on that journey right now. The how is not up to me it is just for me to know that it is real.

The other day as I packed a box I realized how many times have I asked for an adventure in my life -- something fun, something exciting? Here I stand in the middle of it and I just want to say thank you. Rather than being angry about it I want to say thank you, for the grace to move on. Thank you for the sight to see the good in this. Please hear me when I say there have been days I cried more than not. Inside of me is this strength that keeps saying "I will lift up my eyes to the hills from which cometh my help." I stand here with the knowledge that Spirit has opened the windows of heaven and is pouring me out a blessing at this moment. Thank you.

How exciting it is for me to know that my path is divinely guided. I am so very excited to see all of you next weekend at the love and blessing party. I am excited about my trip to NC to spend time with Spirit and my friends there. I am excited to see where my feet take me next. I am excited to talk with anyone and everyone about the goodness I know of the process and the joy cancer has brought into my life. I am excited to be alive, something for so long I took for granted. Each breath I breathe is a gift from the Divine and I am grateful for the gift (present).

My heart is full with love, joy and excitement today. Thank you all for allowing me to share this journey with each of you.

I love you with all my heart.

Your brother and friend

I love you

Allen

I Can Handle A New Growth Experience (I Change)

February 08, 2007 (Personal note from my journal)

I woke up this morning knowing that with growth comes change. Getting the news about my benefits was a day in which I chose to live in fear. Today I know that I don't have to, it is choice. Before me are several options and I am not even there yet. The universe is busy working behind my back for my good as Rev E would say. I have an expectation for Good, Very Good and that is what must show up if I am looking for it. And I am. Being that I have this expectancy, can anything stay the same? Or does change have to happen. I have been asking for a home, a place to call my own, that means I have to move from here. If this is happening soon that means that my home can only be that much closer. I talk about faith in my emails. Is that what everyone is seeing, or fear? It is all a choice.

This is a chance to pay off my debt, clean up my life and prepare for a better day ahead. Just as when I go to Church I get to clean up, put on my best that is what I am doing in my life; Cleaning up for my Good. What is my best friend getting to see each day, Faith or Fear? Not because I am hiding either, I don't want to hide any more I choose LIFE I choose to live transparently. With life comes Change and movement. Thank you for the happiness this morning, for movement in my bones and in my life. I send out Good so Good is what must return to me.

February 23, 2007

I choose Love. It is 2:00 AM and I am awake and feel the need to journal. Yesterday when Paul and I got home from chemotherapy there were several cards from my Mom and Dad's church. Some of them have given me money which is such a blessing and I am so grateful for. The greatest gift I have been given in this journey is my Dad.

I have always known that my dad loves me no matter what has happened. I have chosen pain at times, finding out that when I choose pain it shows up. You know I would never choose to have cancer... but if it has to happen I am so very happy for the wonderful treasures it has given me. My faith, my willingness to let others in, and the love of my dad in a way I have dreamed of all my life.

Thank you for this journey where I get to choose what I take from it. I can choose to look at the pain, the discomfort, being sick, and not wanting to get out of bed. If I do, that will show up, cause that is where my focus would be. However, if I choose love, peace, and blessings, then that is what shows up.

Thank you for Cancer, I bless it and release it. Thank you for the journey in letting others love me. Having Paul, Richard, Ernest, Wayne, my parents, and my countless friends from around the world and the bay area show me love in so many ways. Thank you!

Here am I send me.

I LOVE YOU

Allen

March 2007

I am all packed up and everything I own is in two large storage pods ready to be shipped where I end up at the end of this journey. I have my parents here and we have a party to go to. My friend Lisa, along with many other friends from East Bay, and my life here in the bay area are here to show much love. My mom and dad are seeing just how much I am loved and what a journey this is for us all. Miss Jacque is playing on the piano and the choir is singing and I am filled to full and overflowing. What a way to be sent off in love, what a gift.

How wonderful it is to see how much you are loved and treasured in life while still very much alive. I feel so honored to have all of this love showered over me while I am still here to hear it. Miss Jacque asked me to sing to the group. We agreed on Amazing Grace I cry more than I sing, not tears of sadness, of joy that I am seeing how LOVED I am at this very moment. My parents are crying as they see the love that is being shared with them and the stories of how much I have made a difference in each person's life in this room.

Tomorrow I turn in the keys to the apartment, my folks fly home, I go to chemo, and then I fly to North Carolina. If someone would have told me a year ago this would be happening I would have laughed in their face. "I will never leave CA. NEVER!" Funny thing about never.

Chemo is finished and Antonio and Michael take me to the airport, where we are met by Bob who has clearance for them to roll me to the gate in the chair. I get on the 6 hour flight to NC changing planes in Atlanta only 3 hours from my folks home.

I loved every moment of our visit and I am so happy that I am going to stay with Ern for the next part of this journey. Like clockwork, he is there to meet me at the gate and roll me to the car, take me to his house and allow me to rest for the rest of the day. The next couple days I meet with the new oncologist and we spend time getting to know each other.

Little did I know I was about to learn a couple new dance steps in the dance of life.

Here I am sitting in NC ready to meet the oncologist and knowing that today is going to be a day I get to choose what I hear. In walks this warm, wonderful man and his assistant and we start talking. After 30 minutes he asked me a question that took my breath away. *"What is going on with the spot on your kidney?"* What spot I asked? He said no one has ever mentioned it to you and I say NO!!! He tells me that I have a lump on my kidney and it showed up on the first CT scan and it looked like cancer.

I was speechless and for me that is a big deal. Here I was thinking I had one more treatment and I was going back to CA to resume my life. He suggested that we finish the chemo and see where we were then. I agreed and we set the date for the next treatment. I go in for the next round of Love juice and finish up, go home, all is well. That night Ern and Jim make grilled salmon it was really good going down. The next few days were a dance I remember well. Within 30 minutes of eating I was erupting from both ends at the same time.

Remember that Virgo nightmare earlier; well I have the sequel; Virgo nightmare II.

I am so happy I can laugh about it now. At that moment I ask Ern to run over me with his truck. I had made it through all these treatments of love juice and here I was soiling myself at both ends, now that is some mess. This goes on for the next two days and I go in to see the doctor when my urine turns brown. I have an E Coli infection. What seems like an eternity (which was a couple days) I was feeling better and on the mend. What I know to be my truth today is packing up my life in a box, not knowing what was next, hearing about the spot on my kidney, and living back in the south again. I was choosing to look at the not so good, and it was showing up.

I sat there on Ern's sofa and started my spiritual practices, journaling, setting my intentions, meditating, and within a day my life was so much better.

Tick, tick, tick.

Would I have to have more chemo, was the spot on my kidney gone, was the lymphoma gone, what is next?

The lump was indeed still on my kidney. In my spiritual practice I felt led to move to Seattle, WA which at the time I thought was to be closer to another dear and wonderful friend. I take the rest of the month to gather my strength for the next part of my journey. I am off to the Northwest; here is the Blog Entry for the end of June. I had chosen to see one of the best Urologists in the county and to move to Seattle, WA where I had lived before moving to CA. My friend Richard had helped me find a place near his and the boxes with all my belongings were on their way and so was I.

I was very happy to be on the west coast again, and very happy to have Richard in my life again. Thank you.

June 2007

Hello Family;

I wanted to take some time to share a couple of things with you. One of the many blessings in my life is that the lymphoma is in remission and my new Oncologist is a wonderful man. On my last scan in NC my oncologist there (also very wonderful) had the displeasure of telling me the lump on my kidney was still there. My doctors in CA had thought it to be part of the lymphoma. It was not. They have done more scans and this last week I had MRI's done for 5.5 hours.

Many of you know that I have chosen to hate MRI's and the process. This last week was a true test of my faith and my choice in life. I had many prayers going up for me. I felt them all, thank you! One very wise and special friend reminded me that each click of the MRI was an I love you from the Divine. Thank you for that Lisa. I was able to make a choice to see the MRI in another light. The first 2 hours I was feet first in the MRI chamber of LOVE. I was able to turn my head out and see these 2 wonderful trees. I had to hold my breath as they took scans and each time I did I would look at these trees and they would be swaying in the breeze. I felt peace in knowing that the breath of Spirit was breathing life into them and into me at the same time.

The next day I had to go in head-first; this time for 2.5 hours. Once again I looked for my trees and was able to focus on the breath of the Divine. I was able to feel Choice up close and personal and know that there is nothing that I cannot do with the help of Spirit. I can choose to see good in all things, from chemotherapy to MRI chambers of Love. It is all good.

I received a call from my oncologist last night and the mass on my kidney looks like renal carcinoma which is a type of cancer. Everybody BREATHE!!! The good news is that it can be removed and that is the end of the cancer. I meet with the urologist this week and with the oncologist on Monday. They are also going to be doing a 4 panel CAT scan to look at a spot on my liver. I will be having surgery the end of August or the first of September to remove the growth. I will know more about what all this entails later this next week.

I have my new home in Seattle ready to go and if you need movers I have the best here in Seattle. Thanks to my support team here Richard, Chez and others. I have been able to get it all ready for this next step of the journey. I am choosing PEACE, LOVE, JOY, and WHOLENESS. Spirit is so good.

Please know that I love you all and think of you all the time. I will keep you posted as I know more. I have one request please. When you think of me please CHOOSE to think of me in perfect HEALTH. For that is just where I am. Perfect WHOLE and complete.

With love and gratitude

Your brother and friend Allen Mosley

August 2007

Hello Family

I met with my Urology Team yesterday. Wow how Spirit works!!!!! When I met the first doctor I was distracted by the fact that he was a very handsome person. I love Spirit's humor and way of reminding me that I can choose to look at life anyway I choose.

The meeting went wonderfully, the mass on my kidney has grown and they are 95% sure it is Cancer; the good news is that they are going to try and save the Kidney. They will go in clamp off the kidney and do an ultrasound to make sure they have all the growth. If need be they will remove the entire kidney. The goal is to save as much as they can. Thank you.

I will go in for Surgery on the 5th of September this way I will be able to celebrate my Birthday before I have surgery. Once again the Divine plan is working out. The MRI and the 4 panel CAT scan showed the mass on my liver to be a small growth that they will also look at and remove if they think necessary.

I just want to speak about the divine order of my steps. I really didn't understand why I needed to leave CA and go to NC as I loved my home in CA so very much. I know today that my divine destiny was for me to meet Dr. Orlawski who would tell me about the mass in my kidney and liver. I know today that I needed time to rest and heal. I needed time alone with Spirit to feel the oneness, and know I am one with the Divine I AM. All of my steps are divinely guided. I feel that more today than ever before.

Meeting with the team of doctors that I have now is just so amazing and I feel the presence of the Divine and see it in each and every one of them.

I want you all to know that your prayers, your thoughts, your love, and your support has been a lifeline for me. I see today that each step we take is divinely guided. I urge each of you if you have something in your life that is unresolved with anyone, or anything, to surrender to it. You will find your path to freedom; it will happen. I give thanks for the chance to tell each and every one of you how much I love you, and how grateful I am for the mirror each of you hold for me. I give thanks for the breath, and the knowledge of everyone who is working on my behalf.

Keep holding me in perfect light as I am there. I love you all and can't wait to see you.

All my love Allen

September 02, 2007

Hello my family

I LOVE YOU!!!!!

Be present in all things! Thankful for all things!!!

I received a card today with these words and wanted to share them. I am so very blessed to have each and every one of you in my life. Today I know that the Law of Attraction brings to me those things like me. Thank you. I look at each of you and see the love of Divine, the light of Oneness, and know that Good is in all things.

There is perfect balance in all things.

This next week as I glide through the experience of surgery I know that it is done in perfection and I am in perfect health. I stand in the greatest gift of all, LOVE. I do let the love wash over me, I let it, I let it be.

Take time today to tell those you love just how much you love them. Watch what it does for your heart when you do.

I LOVE YOU VERY MUCH!!!

Your brother and friend Allen Mosley

September 05, 2007

Here I am setting my intention to have no pain and discomfort knowing that the hands of the Divine indeed love me at every step of this journey. There is no difference in today and any other, all is well, and I am whole, perfect, and complete. I am indeed resting in the hands of the Divine all day today, everyday. All is well.

I awake to find Richard in my room. He had been waiting for 8 hours as they removed a third of my kidney and reconnect it to function perfectly. The journey for him was long and he was very happy to see me resting and well. I lay there in the hospital and give great thanks that throughout the last year this is the one time I had been in the hospital overnight. Here I was in a new city with only a couple of friends and yet I knew I was where I was destined to be. I had no idea what was next, yet I knew it would be an adventure in LOVE.

I was very sleepy that evening and slept most of the night. The next morning I was asking what must I do to be discharged? I had to walk, and poo. Might I remind you of my Virgo journey and the joy of laughing at myself. I asked the nurse to help me get this party started. I was up on my feet (barely) with a catheter, 3 drain ports, my back side exposed with an IV pole walking down the hall. Brings a whole new meaning to the word PRETTY! I walked and walked and walked.

The doctor and nurse staff couldn't believe how well I was doing. I told them about writing my intention and part of that was to have no pain and discomfort. I was so pleased I was tender and the thing that was the most irritating was the catheter. I had great fun with it and told everyone I was taking my pee for a walk (Now is a great time to laugh.) Still no poo, they advised me that with eight hours in surgery it would take a while for my internal system to wake up and start to function.

Tick, Tick, Tick

I waited, walked, sat on the throne waiting for the blessed arrival of poo. After two days of walking I awoke the morning of the third day and take my place on the throne and push with all I can. I tell you this to say I never realized how everything inside our bodies is so connected. Something I take so for granted as a BM was the hardest thing I had to do at that moment. With all the moving around they had to do to remove the kidney pushing was shall we say not so very pleasant.

Drum roll please...you got it; here I was so excited about a poo the size of a pea. I called the nurse and told her to call the doctor I was ready to go home. Within hours I was back at home in my apartment sitting and watching TV.

I love you Allen

Chapter Seven:

Living the New Life

Over the next 6 months I would take things one step at a time not lifting over ten pounds, gaining movement more each day. This was the most joyous time on the journey. It was in this time I read every day; I meditated each day, I found the joy of life and living, and was grateful for every leaf on the trees as they changed color, the magic of the first snow and experiencing winter in the northwest. This was a time of deep connection of my internal knowingness, and my connection with the Divine. I took the time to go within and love myself more deeply than I ever had. I took the time to ask myself what I wanted in a relationship, what I wanted in my life, what was my purpose, how to share this journey, and most of all how to thrive in this new way of loving.

In late February I made a conscious decision to surrender the one thing that I had held onto for years. I realized on the journey of the last year plus that I was building a new relationship with myself. I noticed how I had been giving myself away over the years in the name of "pleasure." I knew I wanted something different. If I wanted to thrive in my new life I would need to choose what to do next. I can go back to my old way of living, and attract in more of the same or I can take a new path. I realized that I was getting to know myself for the first time, and I really liked what I was seeing. I kept reading, meditating, loving myself and asking what is next. In meditation I asked my inner self what I wanted. The answer was clear-- to love and appreciate myself in a new way. I had been sexually celibate for the year of treatment and once healed I had returned to the path of old behavior." I woke up and made the conscious decision to date myself for a year. No sex, no dating others, just me. What? Are you crazy, no actually, I am on a quest to honor my divine self and build a relationship with myself that will allow me to thrive in LOVE.

During this time I became ordained and found a new church home, where I began a men's group where we talked about building loving relationships as men. I kept meditating, journaling, writing, and most of all, Loving myself, the real me without all the masks. Funny how, when I took sex out of the equation, I could see more clearly than I had ever before.

I could see the many hidden beliefs around how I had valued myself and took on each one as they arose and asked if they still served me and if not created a new truth for myself. I began to value who I was from the inside out, I began to love who I AM from the inside out. People wanted to date me and know me and I waited. I knew I was on the path to self discovery.

Not only did I love myself I began to like myself. A friend from church, where I was attending told me about a book "5 Love Languages." The journey over the next few months was more alive than the last five years of my life had ever been. I could see finally, my eyes were open. I now knew how to ask for love in a way that I understood. I had a tool that would assist me in loving another more deeply and more authentically that I ever had before. I gleaned the book for everything that served me and started living a life of loving myself deeper than I had dreamed possible.

I was able to ask for what I needed from my friends, my family, and I knew I was ready to open my heart to love. I began to open myself to date and found that with my new glasses I could see more clearly and knew what to look for in myself and what to ask for from others. Most of this journey was being joyous and allowing myself to feel the love from within going out into the world. I was free for the first time in my life. I was living the life I had come here to live. I was creating a life that I wanted to live from the inside out.

I knew for the first time that I had a great deal to offer in a loving relationship and that I mattered. I began to open my heart and allow myself to date. I soon realized that I might have to move and live with friends as my income would not allow me to live alone. I planned to move back to NC where I knew the cost of living was lower and I could continue to recover and create a new life. I had arranged the moving truck, a friend to drive across country with all my things in boxes again.

It was June 2008

My body was healing and life was great, I was emotional about moving back east and yet not knowing what to do other than that. I remember sitting in meditation one day asking what can I do now. Knowing that I was always Divinely guided and this was all for my good. I had resigned myself to living on the east coast again. That Sunday in the middle of service I saw a vision in my thoughts; it was a beautiful man walking into church sitting near the back with this great smile. I heard spirit say this is the person for you, you need to meet him. I thought this is really crazy. I am moving to NC in a few weeks and the boxes are packed ready to go. The end of June was Gay Pride in Seattle and some of my friends needed a ride to service so I arranged to pick them up. Five adults in a VW bug, when the call came in from one of my friends saying I won't be able to meet you, and within seconds another friend called to ask if there was room for an extra person, and I said yes. Best decision of my life.

I get to the pickup spot and the person we are giving a ride to is the most amazing person I have met. Beautiful from the inside out I was so shy I could barely talk. We visited and I was like, this is so not funny God; I am moving to NC and here you are bringing this amazing person into my life. I had planned a trip to CA to visit with my friends there before I moved back to NC and to marry two of my dearest friends. I talked to them about meeting this wonderful man and I had hoped he would email me while I was away. I was disappointed when that didn't happen and was getting ready to head back to Seattle when my friend who was driving me across county said she couldn't drive me. I get back to Seattle all packed up and not knowing what to do next. I check my email and I have a message from Tony, the man in the car. We made arrangements to meet that Sunday at church and have a date afterwards. I was singing and sitting up front when the back door opened and heard that voice again saying, turn around. There on the back row of the church was Tony sitting and smiling at me just as in the vision from before.

My life changed forever that day, we had the most amazing date and we stayed up talking until 2 in the morning. I felt like my heart was going to explode. Within a week Tony suggested there is another path to moving to NC. I could stay with him until I figured it all out. Four years later and counting I am very grateful this Virgo Type A person found my way to Joy and chose a path to love, life, and JOY.

The things that made the greatest difference in my journey to JOY are journaling, meditation, reading books on changing my thoughts, and Spiritual Mind Treatment (affirmative prayer). It is a prayer where I take an active part in what I am calling in. I am asking - believing that what I plant, or leave in the Law of Attraction (Divine) will manifest. Simply put if I plant tomatoes I will get tomatoes, not sweet potatoes.

Today I understand that I can't give out that which I do not hold. In the words of RuPaul 'if you don't love yourself, how the heck you going to love anyone else?" Today I know that my life is a wonderful representation of my "Belief systems" like the roots of a tree firmly planted in the earth, gains its strength, nutrients, and life from that which it is anchored in. The same is true for me and my beliefs, how I love myself, and my being anchored in a life that gives me strength, nourishes me and sustains me. Life is going to show up as life which I now know is a call to my greater yet to be; A time for my abundant well-being to go deeper and find joy in the growth. Most of my life I had spent in the whys.

In life today I know that what shows up in my life is attached in some way to a belief system and some thinking I have been holding onto. "Why" only keeps me longer in the same place. Where do I want to go from here? What do I want in my life? How does it look? How does it feel? What does it smell like? Knowing the things that make me happy and doing those things more and more. I am responsible for my life and how I live it.

The greatest gift I have been given in this journey to joy, this magical walk with the Divine is that I see the good in all paths. I encourage you to find the one that is right for you and follow your heart. Enlightenment, Freedom, Joy, and Peace are an inside job and you are the only one who can give it to you and you alone.

I have the joy of knowing today that I can't help anyone who doesn't want to be helped. I can't help anyone who doesn't ask for help, and I am only responsible for my happiness. You have to find your way there on your own. I find that when I live a life that is happy, joyous, and free I am setting you free to do the same. I guess the best question I asked myself on this journey was, do I want to live?

I realized that if I didn't, I only had to stay on the path I was on, I was taking the fast track to the next existence. If I did want to live, I needed to start where I was and find out where I wanted to go and what I was ready to let go of. Surrender was the gift I found most useful. One of many things I have learned is that when I push, or fight against something or someone it pushes back usually harder and with more force.

When I surrender I relax and let it be knowing that I get to choose how I look at life and can choose with great passion where I want to go. I have not been able to do that while pushing and fighting. I found that in the middle of this journey I was living the life I wanted to all along, a life of freedom, LOVE, and Light. I am happy and all those things I had been working so hard for pushing my way to the top; once I surrendered and started loving myself and others, I have them all.

I have a loving husband, who is the greatest gift of my life. We love and honor each other in new ways. We have a home, that is filled with love and all the things we want, we have a joyous life filled with friends, community, family, abundance, and most of all LOVE. We look for the good in all things and we see it every day. Each day we wake up next to each other is the best day of our lives. I can give you a million why's for my dance with cancer. Today it doesn't matter it showed me the path to loving my body, my life, and a path to JOY.

Thank you

I love you

Rev. Allen Mosley